Richard Reisz
and Bill Grist

TOMORROW'S WORLD

SPACE

GW00566291

BOXTREE

First published in the UK 1994
by BOXTREE LIMITED, Broadwall House,
21 Broadwall, London SE1 9PL

1 3 5 7 9 10 8 6 4 2

Edited by Miranda Smith
Design by Julian Holland Publishing
Artwork by Steve Seymour and Sebastian Quigley
Picture research by Dee Robinson
Cover design by Pinpoint Design Company

1-85283-334-3

Acknowledgements
Boxtree would like to thank Cynthia Page for her help in compiling
the Facts and figures section (pp. 44-47), and Dana Purvis, the
editor of Tomorrow's World for her advice and assistance.

The photographs that appear in the book were obtained from the
following sources:

pp.4-5 NASA; p.6 *above* NASA/Genesis Space Photo Library; p.6
below ESA ERS-1; p.7 *above and below* ESA ERS-1; p.8 *above*
Genesis Space Photo Library; p.8 *below* NASA; p.9 *above* NASA;
p.9 *below* NASDA; p.10 NASA; p.11 *above, left* Frank Spooner
Pictures; p.11 *above, right* NASA; p.11 *below* NASA; p.12 *above*
British Aerospace; p.12 *below* Boeing Defense & Space Group; p.13
above Deutsche Aerospace; p.13 *below* McDonnell Douglas; p.15
left NASA; p.15 *middle and right* NASP; p.17 *above and below left
and right* NASA; p.20 *above* NASA/Pat Rawlings; p.20 *below* NASA;
p.21 *above and below* NASA; p.22 *above* USGS; p.23 *top and middle*
CNES; p.23 *bottom* NASA; p.26 *above, left* NASA; p.26 *above, right*
Novosti (London); p.26 *below* NASA; p.27 *above and below* NASA;
p.28 *above and below* NASA; p.29 *above and below* NASA; p.30
above Peter Menzel/Science Photo Library; p.30 *below* Novosti
(London); p.31 *above* Peter Menzel/Science Photo Library; p.31
below Roger Ressmeyer, Starlight/Science Photo Library; p.34 *above
and below* NASA; p.35 *above and below* NASA; p.36 NASA/Pat
Rawlings; p.37 *above* NASA; p.38 *below* NASA; p.39 *above and
below* NASA; p.40 *below* National Astronomy and Ionosphere
Center, Cornell University; p.41 *above and below* NASA; p.42
David A. Hardy/Science Photo Library; p.43 *above* Julian Baum;
p.43 *below* NASA; p.44 *above and below* NASA; p.45 *left* Novosti
(London); p.46 NASA; p.47 NASA

CONTENTS

INTRODUCTION

THE EXPLOITATION of space has to be counted an astonishing success story. In 1957, a football-sized Russian satellite called Sputnik became the first object manufactured on Earth to go into orbit. As it bleeped its way around the world once every ninety minutes it signalled the dawn of a new era. Today, there are more than 400 working satellites in orbit around our planet, some weighing nearly 20 tonnes. They influence every aspect of our lives. Satellites link our international telephone calls, they relay our television pictures, they provide us with our most accurate systems of navigation, they keep a constant eye on the weather – and networks of military satellites are now on permanent watch high above the Earth. Other orbiting platforms beam down vast quantities of scientific data which are transforming our understanding of the universe and our own planet.

In this remarkable catalogue of achievement in space, manned (and womanned) space flight has so far played a relatively small part. Since the US space agency, NASA, spent $25 billion putting 12 men on the Moon, politicians who have to approve the money for space endeavour, and many scientists too, have been questioning the need to put people into space at all. Almost any space task, except the study of humans themselves, can equally well be done by robots and machines, and at far less cost. And yet, despite the poor returns, and repeated cutbacks in their budgets, crewed space flight programmes are still being funded in Russia, in the USA, in Europe and in Japan.

These programmes have little to do with science, although in time the scientific pay-off should be enormous. The driving force is partly the search for prestige, and the hope that industries will benefit from the new technologies which are developed. It is also partly a belief that space travel has the capacity to inspire us, and particularly the young, as exploration has often done in the past. But all these programmes are also driven by a vision of space as our destiny; by a belief that at some point in the future we will have no option but to expand into space, where energy and mineral resources are more or less infinite.

This book attempts to chart the likely progress of our first tentative steps out into the solar system and beyond. When these missions happen will be a matter for public opinion and governments. That they will happen – eventually – seems to be beyond doubt.

▷ *The repair of the Hubble Space Telescope by astronauts from the Shuttle Endeavour in December 1993 was widely seen as a make or break chance for NASA to demonstrate that people had a useful role in space. The repair, which could not have been completed in any other way, was an outstanding success.*

MISSION TO PLANET EARTH

FOR THE NEXT decade or more, the planet that will come under the closest scrutiny from space is our own. Many of the telescopes and other scientific platforms in orbit now look outwards, their sensors and cameras able to see far more clearly, and further into the depths of space, than is possible from the Earth's surface. But increasingly through the 1990s, scientific satellites will be looking inwards, at the Earth itself. In tune with growing concern about the environment, and aware of the need to show some useful return for their budgets, space agencies are making our home planet their top priority.

The main ambition behind all this effort is to gain a better understanding of the world's climate. In 1991, the European Space Agency launched a satellite, ERS-1, which monitors the Earth in astonishing detail. Among other sophisticated instruments, it uses microwave radar, which can see through clouds and at night, to observe vegetation and crops on land, wind and wave motions at sea, and any changes or cracks in the ice sheets at the poles. It can even measure the temperature of the sea surface to an accuracy of 0.25°C (32.45°F), and variations in sea level to within 10 cm (4 in).

△ *Hurricane Kenneth over the Pacific Ocean in September 1993, seen from the cargo bay of the Shuttle Discovery.*

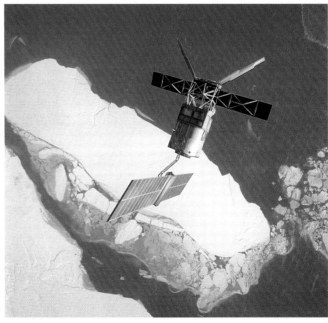

△ *An artist's impression of ERS-1 over the Arctic. The satellite will monitor the state of the ice, and track ice movements.*

ERS-1 was followed into orbit by other more specialised satellites. The American Upper Atmosphere Research Satellite observes processes such as ozone depletion taking place high in the atmosphere, and Topex/Poseidon monitors the oceans with even greater precision than ERS-1. This last satellite is an American/French project, and is producing charts of ocean currents over the whole globe. Ocean currents play a critical role in modifying our climate by transporting heat around the Earth's surface.

Every day, one satellite such as ERS-1 produces enough data about our planet to fill the Encyclopedia Britannica several times over. The amount of information produced by current satellites, however, will be dwarfed by the data from NASA's Earth Observing System planned for the end of the 1990s. This is a whole fleet of orbiting platforms designed to monitor the atmosphere, the oceans and the ground for at least ten years. EOS, as it is known, will produce so much information that designing a system to store the data in a way that allows it to be used is an enormous challenge. The data system being developed for EOS will be the most sophisticated database in the world. Making sense of all the information is going to take many years, but slowly it should begin to fill the many critical gaps in our knowledge of the Earth's climate.

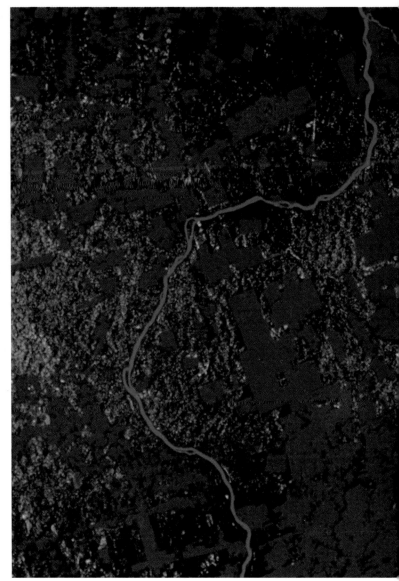

▷ *Amazon rainforest viewed from space by the microwave radar on ERS-1. Forested areas show up as green. The brownish patches are areas of recent deforestation.*

NASA has been keen to demonstrate that the Space Shuttle, and its astronauts, can play a part in all this. Many of the remote sensing instruments used on satellites were developed and tested on board the Shuttle. Several shuttle missions have been dedicated to Earth observation, and used radar and other instruments to monitor Earth resources and the upper atmosphere. In addition, every shuttle mission brings back over 4,000 photographs of the Earth from space, building up a unique record of the processes of change. But the task of observing the Earth in detail over long periods of time is ideally suited to unmanned satellites. People in space will be finding different kinds of work.

◁ *The ocean surface is not flat, but echoes the contours of the sea floor. Topex/Poseidon can monitor even smaller variations in the surface height caused by ocean currents.*

MADE IN SPACE

SOME DAY, space factories are likely to make use of the abundant solar energy in orbit to produce a range of materials that are difficult, or even impossible, to make on Earth. For almost 20 years, astronauts have carried out experiments in the near-zero gravity conditions in orbit known as microgravity, in the search for drugs, semiconductors, and new structural materials which it might soon be profitable to manufacture in space.

◁ *Space Station Mir viewed from a departing Soyuz spacecraft. The materials laboratory Kristall is the module to the left of the picture.*

The closest thing to a space factory so far is Mir, Russia's permanently manned outpost in space. Through Mir, and an earlier series of smaller space stations called Salyut, the Russians have gained unmatched experience of both long duration space flight and space manufacture. Since the core module was launched in 1986, Mir has been growing into a space complex as modules are attached.

One module called Kristall is dedicated to research into materials and is now operating as a pilot production plant for semiconducting crystals, such as gallium arsenide. These crystals, used for the manufacture of microchips, can be grown in space with far fewer of the faults and stresses that gravity induces.

Mir has also produced hundreds of kilograms of strong, lightweight metallic composites, which are much tougher if they can be produced free of imperfections. To cope with the scale of space production on Mir, the unmanned tanker Progress M has been used to ferry the samples back to Earth.

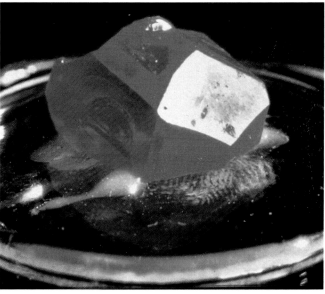

△ *A crystal of mercuric oxide grown in April 1985 aboard Spacelab, a European module carried in the Shuttle's cargo bay.*

The most promising American experiment in space manufacture in the early 1980s used a technique called electrophoresis to purify drugs. An electric field can separate a drug in solution from any contaminants because of the different electric charges they carry. On Earth, convection currents limit the purity which can be achieved. However, in the last few years this method of producing drugs has been rapidly overtaken by new laboratory techniques – particularly genetic engineering. Space scientists now consider that the best prospect for microgravity research is the crystallisation of proteins. The X-ray diffraction patterns produced by protein crystals show their three dimensional structure. This allows drugs to be manufactured which either mimic the protein's action, or stop it from working. The larger, high quality crystals which can be grown in space should greatly improve this process.

Although some early experiments have proved disappointing, much more research is planned. Scientists hope, for instance, to crystallise an enzyme from the virus HIV to help in the development of an AIDS drug. This kind of research to improve Earth-based techniques might be the best use of microgravity in the short term. People have been investigating how materials behave in different conditions of pressure and temperature for hundreds of years, but they have only just begun to look at the effects of switching off gravity!

△ Crystals grown on the Space Shuttle of the protein phospholipase, a cell enzyme often found in snake venom.

◁ HOPE, Japan's unmanned shuttle, is planned as an advanced microgravity laboratory. It will be launched on the country's powerful new H-II rocket.

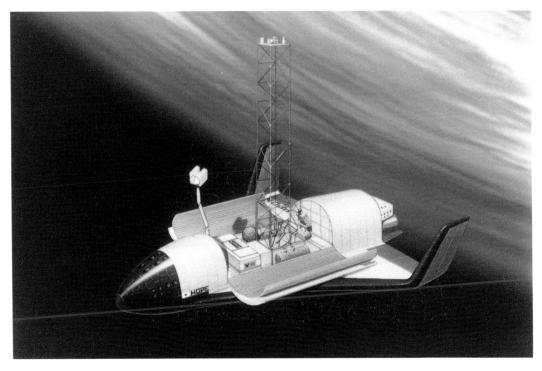

In Japan, space plans being considered for the 1990s include the use of tax incentives to encourage the large-scale industrialisation of space – for instance, to manufacture new alloys from metals which will not mix properly on Earth because of their different densities.

Work has already started on an unmanned shuttle, HOPE, which early in the next century, could be supplying the Japanese module on the international space station (see page 10), and acting as a free-flying platform for advanced microgravity research.

STEPPING STONE TO SPACE

NOTHING ILLUSTRATES the changing attitudes to manned space flight better than the history of the US Space Station Freedom. Announced in 1984 by President Reagan as the next great space adventure, Freedom was to be both an international orbiting laboratory, and a staging post for manned missions to the Moon, Mars and beyond. As costs have risen, the design has been repeatedly simplified, and the project has come close to being cancelled several times. The latest plans are so far short of the original that even the name has been changed. Freedom has become Alpha.

Despite the cut-backs, the Americans have been careful to make sure that Alpha can still include the major elements of the space station being designed by other space agencies. Europe and Japan are each building a laboratory module, and Canada is developing a robotic arm to help assemble and repair the structure. In addition, the new plans have a role for the Russians. NASA would like to use some of the well-tested Russian hardware, including the Soyuz spacecraft which could function as Alpha's space lifeboat – a vehicle to return the crew to Earth in an emergency.

◁ The ever-shrinking international Space Station Alpha. Two Soyuz 'lifeboats' can be seen attached to the habitation module at the top of the picture. The other three large modules are the laboratories.

The suggestion is that assembly of Alpha in orbit would begin in 1996, with the amount of construction necessary in space kept to a minimum. From 1997, astronauts should be able to spend periods of up to two weeks living in the Shuttle and working in the US laboratory module. By 2001, a crew of four could be based on Alpha permanently. The crew would live in the habitation module where each astronaut has their own small cabin, with a sleeping bag stuck to the wall to prevent it floating away, and a personal workstation linked to Alpha's central computer. There is also a communal cooking and eating area, space in which to exercise and carry out medical checks – and of course the zero gravity showers and toilets.

The habitation module is linked to the three laboratory modules where the scientific work would be done. NASA has been directed to give top priority on the space station to research into the effects of long-term space flight. Many of the changes which occur in weightless conditions, like the loss of bone density, are similar to the effects of normal ageing and it is hoped that studying these processes will be of value to us all.

Alpha would also carry a large number of general microgravity experiments. These would include biological experiments on improved cell growth in near-weightless conditions. This could prove important in cancer research, and in the production of new tissues and organs for transplants.

△ A mock-up of the crew compartments with fixed sleeping bags and personal workstations.

△ The habitation module mock-up with accommodation for eight. The real thing will now be much smaller.

◁ A proposed Space Station combining Alpha and the Russian Mir 2 would have 25 per cent more space than Alpha. To assemble all the components, 31 launches of Russian, American and European spacecraft would be needed.

Not surprisingly, as the space station has shrunk, its suitability as a base for everything from space exploration to science has been reduced. Many scientists who supported Freedom think that the Alpha design is one cutback too many, and NASA has now has come up with another plan. In 1996, the Russian Space Agency had intended to launch a new space station known as Mir 2. Both space agencies have now proposed that Alpha and Mir 2 be combined into a new space station – the Russian Alpha or R-alpha! The attractions of the idea are clear. R-alpha will accomodate a crew of six instead of four, it will be completed sooner and it will cost less. It will also demand a level of international scientific collaboration which is unprecedented. Whether all of the partners, from East or West, are ready to cooperate on such a scale remains to be seen.

TOWARDS A SPACE BUS

NASA'S REUSABLE SPACE Shuttle was intended to reduce the cost of launching payloads into orbit. In fact, the system is so complex, and safety precautions for the crew are so demanding, that Shuttle launch costs are actually greater than with conventional throwaway rocket boosters. It costs over $20,000 to put one kilogramme into orbit on the Shuttle. Several launch systems now on the drawing-board or in development promise a reduction in launch costs of at least 90 per cent. They use new lightweight structural materials, in some cases completely new types of engine, and all are completely reusable.

△ *The 'interim' HOTOL immediately after separation from the Antonov AN-225 heavy lift aircraft.*

The UK's HOTOL, announced in 1984, was conceived as a one-stage spaceplane which would take off from a runway, boost itself into orbit, and then fly back down to Earth and land like an aircraft. It was based on a revolutionary hybrid engine which was to be part jet and part rocket. Initial studies of both the engine and spacecraft were promising but have now been run down, and British Aerospace is now proposing an 'interim' vehicle built around existing engine technology. The project, developed jointly with the Russians, would use the world's largest aircraft, an Antonov 225, to lift HOTOL to an altitude of 9 km (6 miles). From there, HOTOL would use rocket engines to propel itself and a payload of up to 8 tonnes into orbit before returning to Earth. Early versions would be unmanned, although the vehicle could in time be adapted to carry crew to the space station. It could also evolve into a vehicle capable of taking off from the ground once the hypersonic hybrid engine is developed.

Several other two-stage spaceplanes have been proposed. One concept recently unveiled by the US company Boeing could be built using existing technology.

△ *Boeing's two-stage-to-orbit concept. The company claims it could be flying by the year 2002.*

In the Boeing design a rocket-powered orbiter would be launched from a large supersonic carrier as big as a Boeing 747. The orbiter would be slung below the mothership. The company thinks this is a simpler and more efficient arrangement than the piggy-back design favoured by others, such as the German Sanger.

Sanger is an ambitious proposal, which would require the development of advanced turbo-ramjets, so far used only on certain types of missile. The ramjets would accelerate the first pilotless stage to speeds of more than Mach 6, and an altitude of 35 km (22 miles). A rocket-powered second stage – which could be manned or unmanned – would continue into orbit. The designers are optimistically suggesting that, in order to spread the costs, the first stage could also be developed as a hypersonic aircraft.

▷ *The German designed Sanger's second stage accelerates away from the hypersonic mothercraft at an altitude of 35 km (22 miles).*

Already off the drawing-board is a reusable single stage rocket being funded by the US military. Using advanced materials, and highly efficient but conventional rocket engines, it is designed to reach space in one stage, and then to turn round and come back again.

A one-third scale prototype of the rocket, called the DC-X, has already flown. In the summer of 1993, it took off from the White Sands Missile Range in New Mexico, hovered and manoeuvred sideways 100 m (328 ft) above the ground, and then settled back down on its landing pad. Further tests with a prototype twice the size should see sub-orbital flights reaching a height of 150 km (94 miles). If tests continue to go well, the full-sized orbiter, the DC-1, could be flying by the end of the century.

◁ *The historic first flight of the DC-X, the world's first completely reusable rocket. A recent NASA study suggested this might well be the best concept for the next generation of launcher, replacing the Shuttle for human space flight.*

THE X-30

S EVERAL COUNTRIES already have designs for the space vehicles of the 21st century: aerospaceplanes. These are one-stage winged vehicles which, like the original HOTOL, would fly both in the atmosphere and up into space. The most advanced of these projects is the US National Aerospace Plane (NASP). Since 1986, NASA and the US Airforce have been developing the technology necessary to build a prototype known as the X-30. The next stage of this project aims to build an unmanned hypersonic vehicle to test the X-30's engines in flight. The engines are of a new type known as supersonic ramjets, or scramjets, which could take the craft close to its orbital velocity of Mach 25. Additional rocket engines, for which liquid oxygen would have to be carried on board, should be needed only for the final push into space.

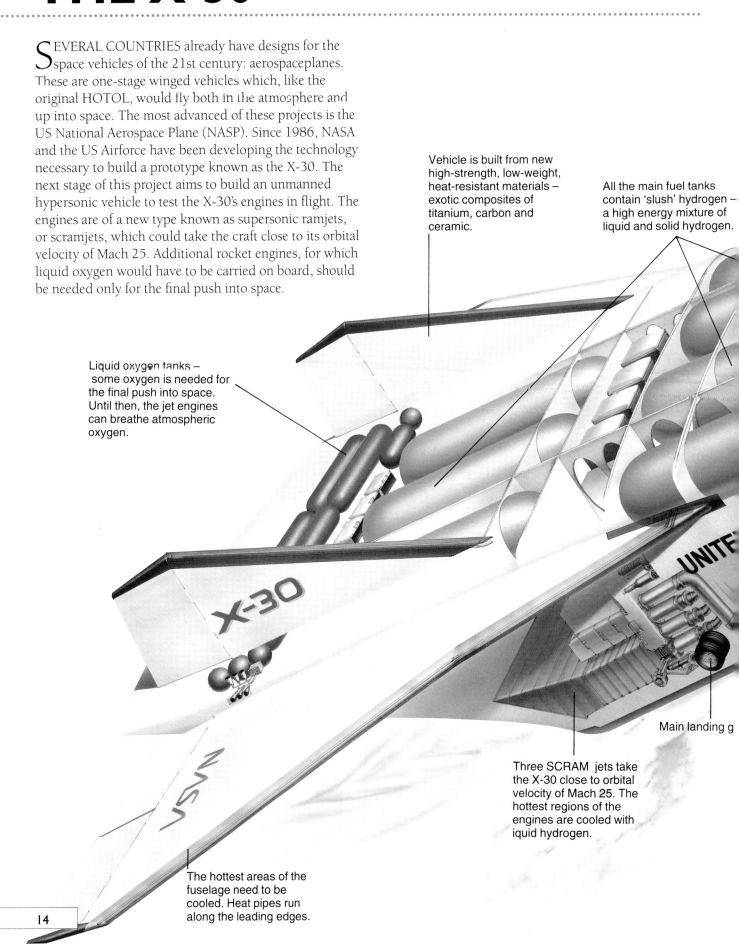

Vehicle is built from new high-strength, low-weight, heat-resistant materials – exotic composites of titanium, carbon and ceramic.

All the main fuel tanks contain 'slush' hydrogen – a high energy mixture of liquid and solid hydrogen.

Liquid oxygen tanks – some oxygen is needed for the final push into space. Until then, the jet engines can breathe atmospheric oxygen.

Main landing g

Three SCRAM jets take the X-30 close to orbital velocity of Mach 25. The hottest regions of the engines are cooled with liquid hydrogen.

The hottest areas of the fuselage need to be cooled. Heat pipes run along the leading edges.

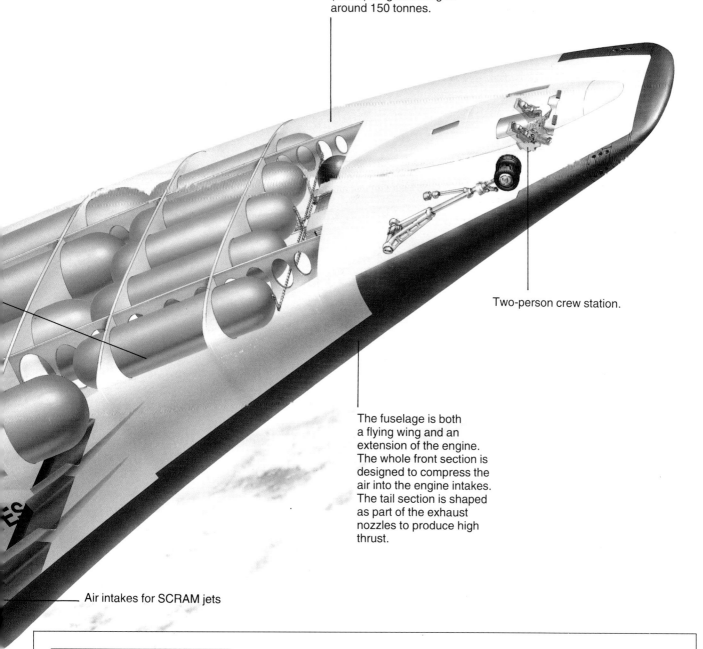

The X-30 is about 55 m (180 ft) long and weighs around 150 tonnes.

Two-person crew station.

The fuselage is both a flying wing and an extension of the engine. The whole front section is designed to compress the air into the engine intakes. The tail section is shaped as part of the exhaust nozzles to produce high thrust.

Air intakes for SCRAM jets

The X-30 airframe has been designed and tested inside supercomputers. Wind tunnels are unable to simulate the enormous pressures and temperatures encountered at speeds of more than eight times the speed of sound.

The exhaust plume at Mach 10

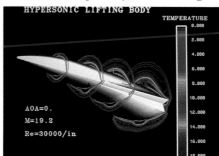

Temperatures generated around the X-30 at very high velocity.

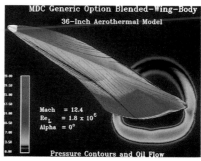

Air flow around the vehicle, showing areas of high drag

ELEVATORS IN SPACE

SINCE THE 1950S, space scientists have been discussing structures which sound like science fiction: elevators in space. If a space station in a high orbit is tied or tethered to a space port in an orbit 100 km (63 miles) or so below, then elevators could run up and down the cables between the two. A spacecraft launched from Earth need only reach the port in low orbit; from there its cargo could continue the journey upwards in a lift, with enormous savings in energy. And, although it may sound like fantasy, tethered spacecraft have already been tested.

The theory of space tethers is straightforward. A satellite in low orbit has to travel faster than one in a higher orbit. As a result, if the two satellites are linked together, the lower one will be slowed down and will have to be supported by the tether, while the higher one will be accelerated and strain outwards on the tether like a stone swung round on the end of a string. The system as a whole should remain in a stable orbit with the cable between the satellites pulled taut.

Tethers between spacecraft could have a number of surprising applications besides space elevators. For instance, if a satellite was reeled out on the end of a tether from the Space Shuttle and then released, it would be flung into a higher orbit as if from a sling.

Alternatively, tethers could be used to generate power. A tethered cable cutting through the Earth's magnetic field will, like a dynamo, generate an electrical voltage. A tether 100 km (63 miles) long should be able to provide the Shuttle with the 40 kilowatts of electrical power it needs. The energy has to come from somewhere, and in fact the Shuttle's orbit would slowly decay, but on short missions this would not matter. For longer missions, say on the space station, the system could be used as an energy store. While the space station was shielded from the Sun it could take energy from the tether, with a slight decay of the orbit. When it was back in sunlight, the solar panels could put energy into the tether which would have the effect of pumping up the station's orbit again. So the station can use its own orbit, instead of batteries, to store electrical power. In much the same way, a tether could be used to adjust the orbit of a spacecraft, up or down, with no need to use propellant.

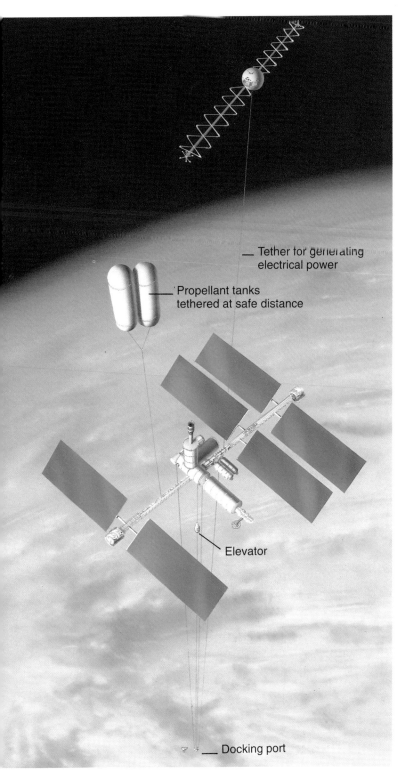

— Tether for generating electrical power

Propellant tanks tethered at safe distance

Elevator

Docking port

◁ *Tethers in use on a space station. The docking port connected by elevator is unlikely to be built in the near future, but the others could well be deployed by Space Station Alpha.*

In the 1960s, early experiments with tethers showed that the orbital mechanics were more complicated than people had realised. After a 30 m (98 ft) Dacron strap unexpectedly gyrated like a skipping rope, NASA decided to leave tethers alone until the phenomenon was better understood. It was not until 1992, after extensive rehearsal in supercomputers, that they dared to try again. This time a Shuttle attempted to reel out a satellite known as TSS on a 20 km (12½ miles) cable to experiment with generating power, and to see if the behaviour of the tether had been correctly predicted. It had not, and the reel mechanism jammed four times as the tether was spooled out just 260 m (853 ft).

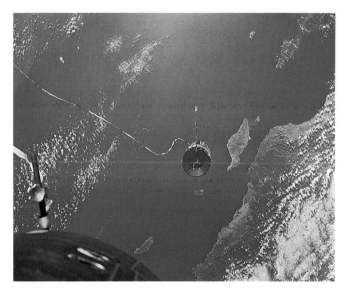

▷ *In 1966, the gyrations of a tether between Gemini XI and the Agena upper stage were not predicted at all.*

Since then, NASA has returned to basics and in 1993 successfully deployed 20 km (12½ miles) of polythene fibre from a satellite to study the tether's motions. In time, the earlier Shuttle mission will be attempted again, and the next step has already been planned. A satellite on a long line below the Shuttle will be dragged through the upper atmosphere. There, it will take measurements in a region 100-200 km (62-125 miles) high – too high for balloons, too low for orbiting spacecraft – that only a tether can reach.

▽ *A planned future mission for TSS. On a 100 km (62 mile) tether below the Shuttle, the satellite gathers data from the Earth's upper atmosphere.*

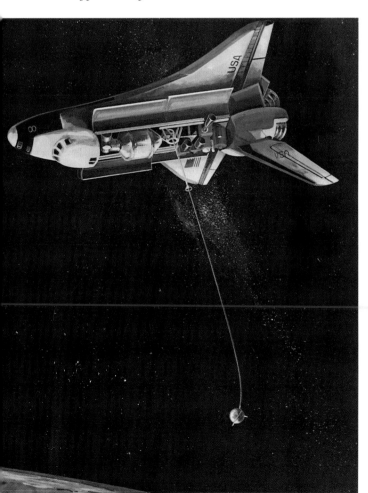

▽ *Space Shuttle Atlantis attempts to reel out the tethered Italian satellite TSS. An unknown phenomenon caused the reeling mechanism to jam, but the satellite's thrusters were successful in damping out vibrations in the tether.*

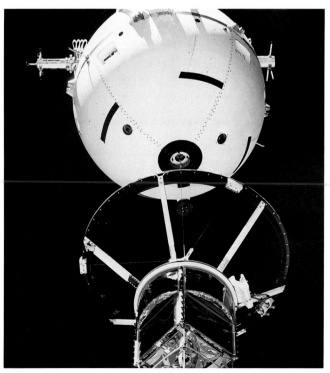

MOONBASE

SINCE 1986, NASA has been refining plans for a permanent base on the surface of the Moon, although when it happens the cost makes it likely that it will become an international venture. Initially, a habitat module would accommodate a crew of four for stays of around two weeks. Then, as the frequency of flights and the length of time on the surface increased, the base would expand, possibly by linking together a series of modules, or by landing one large inflatable habitat. By the year 2010, a crew of twelve could be based on the lunar surface for periods of up to a year in a base looking something like this.

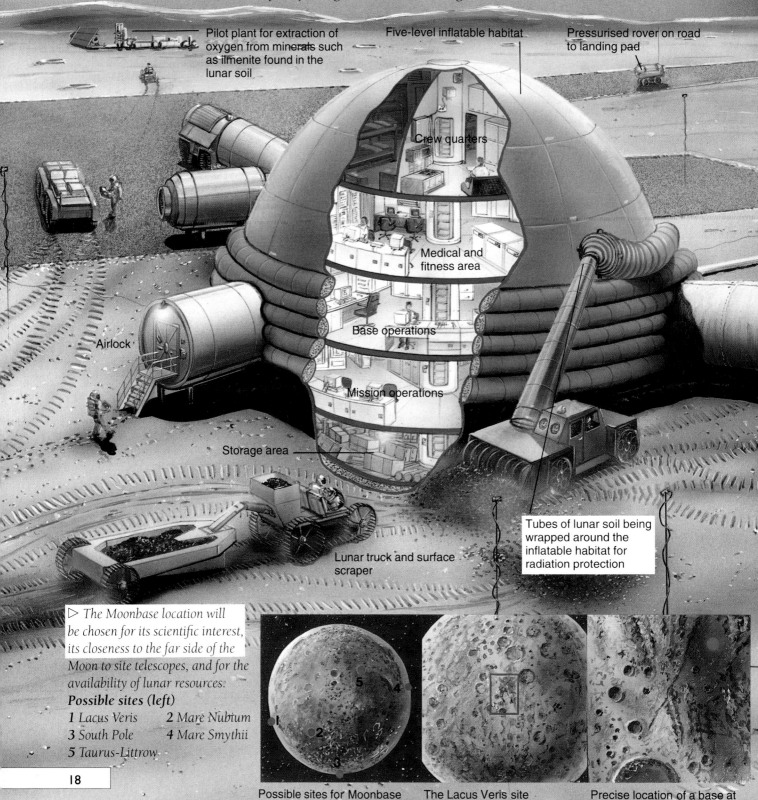

Pilot plant for extraction of oxygen from minerals such as ilmenite found in the lunar soil

Five-level inflatable habitat

Pressurised rover on road to landing pad

Crew quarters

Medical and fitness area

Base operations

Mission operations

Airlock

Storage area

Tubes of lunar soil being wrapped around the inflatable habitat for radiation protection

Lunar truck and surface scraper

▷ *The Moonbase location will be chosen for its scientific interest, its closeness to the far side of the Moon to site telescopes, and for the availability of lunar resources.*

Possible sites (left)

1 *Lacus Veris*   2 *Mare Nubium*
3 *South Pole*   4 *Mare Smythii*
5 *Taurus-Littrow*

Possible sites for Moonbase   The Lacus Veris site   Precise location of a base at

◁ A landing craft being unloaded into a pressurised rover. The landing site would be about 2.5 km (1.5 miles) away to reduce dust and chemical contamination of the base.

100 kW solar power system with fuel cells for night storage

Original module with shielding used as construction shack

LUNAR AMBITIONS

'BACK TO THE MOON, back to the future, and this time back to stay.' In July 1989, twenty years after the first manned landing on the Moon, the then President of the United States, George Bush, made his famous commitment to lunar exploration. The Moon will be of enormous interest in its own right, but the plan was also to use the Moon as a step towards Mars, with the aim of mounting a crewed mission to the red planet within 30 years. The Moon would provide valuable experience of working on an alien world in low gravity conditions. The spacecraft and habitats designed for the Mars expedition could be tested on the Moon, and a full-scale rehearsal of the whole mission could be undertaken, with rescue by the Moonbase crew possible at any time if something should go wrong.

△ A Mars landing is rehearsed on the Moon. Astronauts set up equipment unloaded from the Mars lander.

The initial functions of a Moonbase would be largely scientific. A study of the Moon's cratered terrain gives geologists a unique record of the origins and violent history of the Earth-Moon system. Expeditions lasting several weeks to gather geological samples could range up to 3,000 km (1,875 miles) from the base in trains of pressurised rovers. Excursions further afield could be done in sub-orbital hops by the lunar landing craft.

▷ A survey team deep drilling for core samples in the 4 km (2¹/₂ mile) deep impact crater, Aristarchus.

One of the earliest tasks of scientists on the Moon would be to assemble a radio telescope. From the stable, airless lunar surface, astronomers should be able to peer deeper into space than ever before. The low gravity conditions are ideal for the construction of large instruments, and the radio telescope would be followed by optical, gamma ray and other telescopes. On the Moon's far side these would be shielded from interference from Earth.

▷ *An observatory on the far side of the Moon. The large radio telescope is set into an existing crater.*

A crew based on the lunar surface could investigate the Moon's wealth of natural resources. Metallic oxides in the soil could be processed to provide oxygen for life support and fuel. Since Moon dust also contains small amounts of hydrogen, absorbed over billions of years from the solar wind, eventually all the rocket fuel needed for space exploration could be obtained from the lunar surface. In time, lunar ores could be mined on a commercial scale for the minerals they hold – silicon, iron, aluminium, titanium.

Materials mined on the Moon could be transported back to Earth in low speed freighters (see p.36-7). The trip might take several months, but the freighters could carry over 100 tonnes of lunar material at a time.

The lunar soil also contains helium-3, which is absorbed like hydrogen from the solar wind. Extremely rare on Earth, helium-3 is potentially a 'clean' fuel for fusion reactors. If such reactors are successfully developed, one craft the size of the Space Shuttle could ferry back enough lunar helium-3 to meet the whole of Earth's energy needs for a month!

If a scientific base is not established on the Moon by the international community early in the next century, it is possible that commercial interests will get there first. The Japanese have made no secret of the fact that a long-term aim of their space programme is to gain access to the mineral riches of the Moon, and help make good their country's lack of natural resources. As yet, there is no international agreement on ownership of the Moon's minerals, and some kind of international 'lunar treaty' will be needed if the Moon's wealth is to benefit the Earth as a whole.

◁ *A lunar resource mining base. The rail gun can accelarate payloads of minerals or liquid oxygen to high speed, and fire them into lunar orbit.*

THE RED PLANET

FOR SPACE SCIENTISTS, Mars, the planet most like Earth in the solar system, has a special fascination. Budgets may be cut and missions may be trimmed, but during the 1990s Russia, Japan, the United States and Europe are all planning to send probes to the red planet. These missions will explore Mars – above, on and below the surface – and are essential preparation before any manned exploration can be attempted.

▷ *In 1976, the Viking orbiters sent back stunning pictures of the Martian surface which revealed a planet which once had glaciers, rivers, and even oceans. Shallow seas in this canyon, the Valles Marineris, might once have harboured life.*

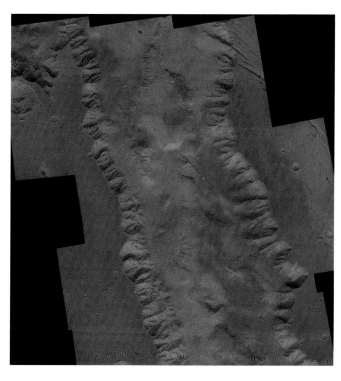

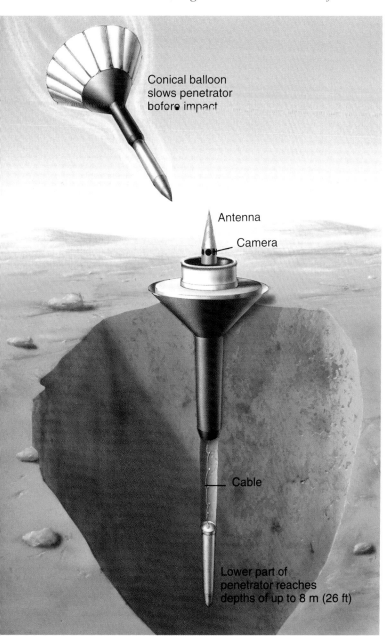

Conical balloon slows penetrator before impact

Antenna

Camera

Cable

Lower part of penetrator reaches depths of up to 8 m (26 ft)

This focus on Mars began with disappointment when contact was lost with the US Mars Observer probe in 1993, as it was about to begin a detailed survey of the Martian surface. But US space scientists hope to launch a follow-up craft known as Mars Surveyor in 1996. And in the same year, another mission, led by Russia with European and US involvement, is due to set off for the planet. Called Mars '96, it will survey Mars from orbit and send four probes with cameras down to the surface. These probes include surface weather stations which can also analyse the soil around them, and penetrators, designed to tunnel into the Martian terrain on impact. Whilst the top portion of the penetrator lodges on the surface, the lower section buries itself up to 8 m (26 ft) into the ground. The penetrators will analyse the composition of the Martian soil, and look for water. How much water remains on Mars, and at what depth, is fundamental to the prospects for human exploration.

◁ *The Mars penetrators will hit the surface at speeds approaching 360 km/h (225 mph) allowing them to penetrate even into rock. The surface portion will relay the data to the orbiter.*

The Americans are also considering a mission called Pathfinder which would land a surface station on the planet and is seen as the first in a series of low cost sorties leading to a network of stations on the Martian surface by early next century. With the European Space Agency also developing its own plans for Mars exploration and the Russians planning a follow-up to Mars '96, there could be considerable duplication of effort, and the world's space agencies have now agreed to cooperate over Mars exploration.

The first test of this cooperation could come in 1998 in a mission known as 'Mars Together'. 'Mars Together' would be a joint Russian/US/European space flight, and is daringly ambitious. As the probe goes into orbit around Mars it will release a descent module which will fall towards the surface. High in the atmosphere, the module will split into two capsules. The first containing a Russian-built surface rover will continue its descent by parachute. When it reaches the surface this rover, responding to general directions from Earth, will rely on its own systems to avoid obstacles and navigate. Over two years it will cover up to 100 km (63 miles) of Martian territory, sending back panoramic photographs of the surface. It may also carry a much smaller US-designed mini-rover to study the surface even more closely.

The other capsule will contain a package which, as it falls through the Martian atmosphere, will suddenly begin to inflate, until after five minutes, it has become a gigantic helium-filled balloon. Below the balloon will be a gondola containing instruments and a camera, and below that a long titanium tail called a snake. For about two weeks, the balloon will drift in the wind around Mars taking detailed pictures and travelling several hundred kilometres a day. At night, as the helium cools, it will descend to the surface until the snake is dragging on the ground. Instruments in the snake will then collect information about the soil in that particular location. The next day, as the balloon warms, it will take to the air again and continue its Martian tour.

If 'Mars Together' is a success, the next international mission could be to return a sample of Martian soil to Earth. This is regarded as a necessary rehearsal for sending a crew to Mars as it involves successfully landing a spacecraft on the planet, and then bringing it back. A sample from Mars would also help to define the scientific goals of a manned mission. Combined with the results of all the Martian surveys, it would allow detailed preparation for this next big step in human spaceflight to begin.

▷ *The Russian-built Mars rover 'Marsokhod', in trials in Death Valley, California. Its six wheels and jointed chassis allow it to negotiate the most difficult terrain.*

△ *The gigantic balloon to be carried by Mars Together will be filled with 5,500 cubic metres (194,000 cubic feet) of helium.*

▽ *In California's Mojave Desert the 'snake' demonstrates how it can slither over the surface without snagging.*

MISSION TO MARS

IN 1991, a committee of American space experts, drawn
from NASA and industry, came up with a set of
recommendations for the best way to achieve the target of
a manned mission to Mars. They strongly advised using a
nuclear rocket for the trip. This allows propellant to be
used much more efficiently, and reduces the journey time
and the risks to the astronauts of being in deep space (see
pp.26-27). The cost of the mission has been estimated at
anywhere between $50 billion and a staggering $500
billion. NASA has now accepted that it is unlikely
America will ever go it alone. With so much interest in
the planet, it seems probable that building the proposed
Mars ship would become a global project.

Interplanetary
Mission module.
A five-level habitat
to accommodate the
crew during the long
journey to and from
Mars.

Stowage deck

Crew sleeping
quarters

The Mars ship would
be over 100 m (328 ft)
long and weigh 650
tonnes. It would have
to be accombled in
Earth orbit.

Cargo pods

Mars Excursion
Module – a two-stage
lander for descent to
Mars surface, and
return to Mars orbit.

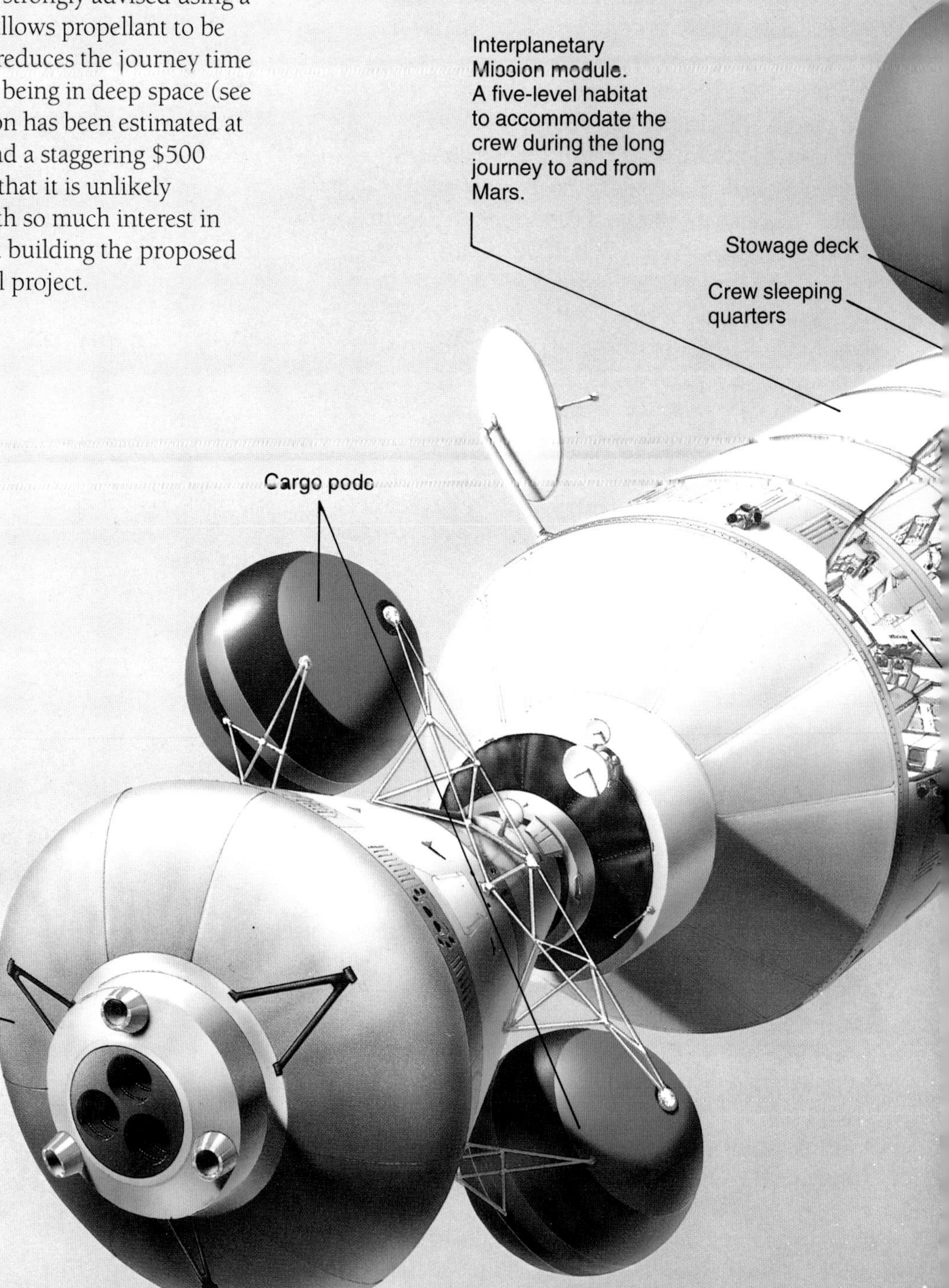

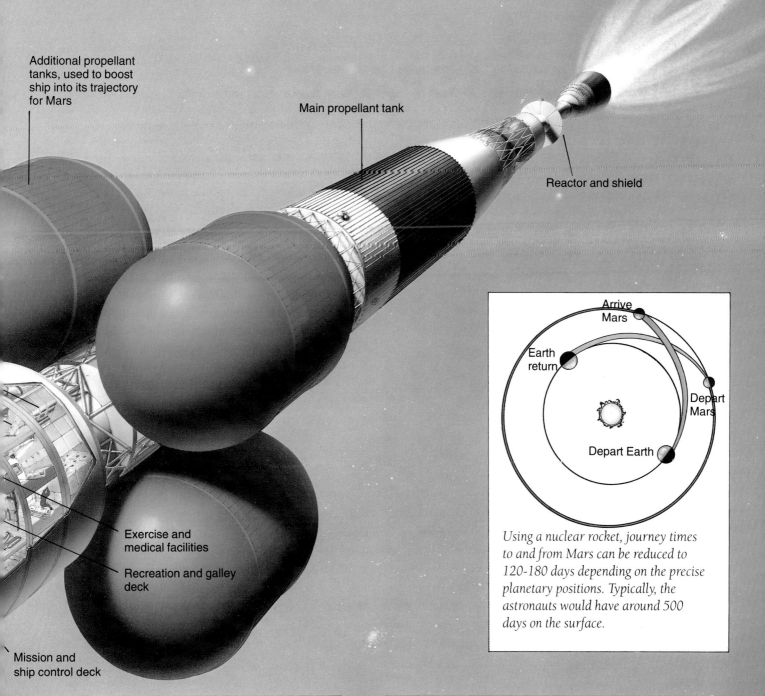

Additional propellant tanks, used to boost ship into its trajectory for Mars

Main propellant tank

Reactor and shield

Exercise and medical facilities

Recreation and galley deck

Mission and ship control deck

Arrive Mars

Earth return

Depart Mars

Depart Earth

Using a nuclear rocket, journey times to and from Mars can be reduced to 120-180 days depending on the precise planetary positions. Typically, the astronauts would have around 500 days on the surface.

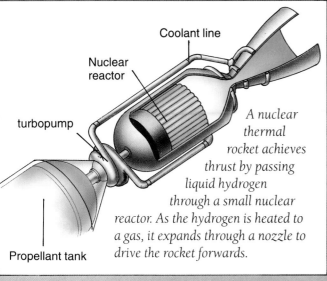

Coolant line

Nuclear reactor

turbopump

Propellant tank

A nuclear thermal rocket achieves thrust by passing liquid hydrogen through a small nuclear reactor. As the hydrogen is heated to a gas, it expands through a nozzle to drive the rocket forwards.

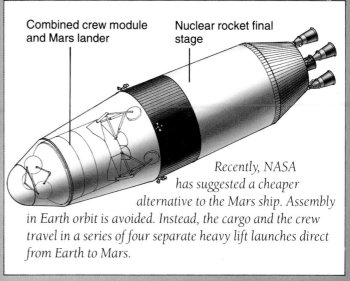

Combined crew module and Mars lander

Nuclear rocket final stage

Recently, NASA has suggested a cheaper alternative to the Mars ship. Assembly in Earth orbit is avoided. Instead, the cargo and the crew travel in a series of four separate heavy lift launches direct from Earth to Mars.

LIVING IN SPACE

WHILE FLOATING in space may be great fun, it is not without danger. Many of the systems that control the composition of our bodies and its ability to renew itself are confused by weightlessness. Also, without the physical strains of our daily battle with gravity, the human body can literally waste away. The Russians have the greatest experience of the effects of long periods in space. Two cosmonauts spent over a year there, and future plans include a two-year stay in space the time that even the shortest Mars mission would take. Without gravity, all the muscles of the body, including the heart, begin to waste away. The current solution is exercise. On Mir, the cosmonauts work out regularly, and wear special suits that are stiffened to make physical movement harder, so that the body is exercised throughout the day. Recent evidence from Mir suggests that with these precautions changes to the heart muscle take place in the first two or three months in space and then a new equilibrium is reached. With enough exercise, a crew should be able protect themselves from muscle wastage even on a long journey to Mars.

△ In space, exercise can overcome some but not all of the negative effects of weightlessness.

△ Yuri Romanenko spent 326 days in space. Without gravity he had grown 10 cm (4 in).

A more threatening physical change to an astronaut is the weakening of bones. This is not simply a physical effect caused by a lack of exercise in a weightless environment. Lack of gravity actually reduces the body's ability to absorb calcium from food and makes it excrete calcium faster than it would on Earth. Unfortunately, calcium supplements in the food and regular exercise do not completely solve the problem. To do so, it will probably be necessary on a long flight to create artificial gravity by spinning the spacecraft, or a small centrifuge could be carried to spin each crew member for a short period every day. The Russians have shown that this works with rats, but it may not be popular with a human crew.

▷ Astronaut Mae Jennison enjoying weightlessness aboard the Space Shuttle Endeavour.

Another serious danger on any venture into deep space is the threat of high energy particles produced by flares on the Sun. The Earth's magnetic field provides some protection for spacecraft in near-Earth orbit, but in empty space the stream of protons emitted by a large flare could be fatal. So a small unmanned satellite will be positioned close to the Sun to give a few minutes warning of larger, life-threatening flares. The astronauts would then have time to retreat to a small, heavily-shielded room at the heart of the craft for the duration of the solar storm.

▷ *In the early days of space travel the food was dull and tasteless, but now the Shuttle meals are tasty and varied.*

Apart from the physical stress the astronauts will face during any mission into deep space, there is the mental strain. For the long trip to Mars, the crew will be chosen partly for their psychological qualities. However, problems have arisen in the past. On a Russian Salyut mission in 1985 the station commander Vladimir Vasyutin became withdrawn, tired and uninterested in work. Ground control decided he was suffering from a nervous breakdown and aborted the mission.

To reduce stress, the interior of the ship will be as 'homely' as possible, but it may not be possible to include windows. Here, technology may have the answer. Flat-screen video windows could provide a view of whatever the crew members wish to see, or a real view could be relayed from an outside camera. Boredom will be another factor, and virtual reality may provide one solution to this. Astronauts will be able to 'visit' a virtual Earth, play games, or cycle through a virtual landscape to relieve the tedium of their cramped craft.

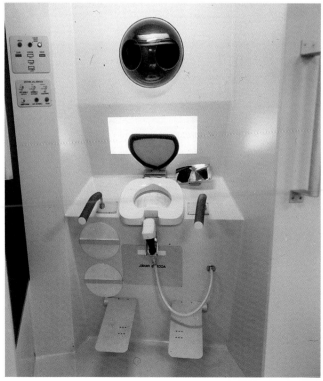

▷ *A zero gravity toilet cunningly uses air suction to solve one of the many problems of weightlessness.*

ON THE MARTIAN SURFACE

IN 1976, the Viking 1 lander became the first object from Earth to land on the surface of Mars. The information it relayed back showed that the conditions there are incredibly hostile to life as we know it. The temperature averages –60°C (–76°F), and the atmosphere is composed largely of carbon dioxide. Each Viking lander carried three experiments to test the Martian soil for signs of life. While two of the experiments were negative, the third gave an ambiguous result. However, it is now widely believed that there is no life on Mars.

◁ *Our first close look at the surface of another planet. Taken just 24 hours after landing, the foot of Viking 1 is seen at the bottom of the frame.*

△ *In NASA's latest plans for the first landing on Mars, the crew of six will spend 500 days in these two living habitats.*

The first manned mission to the red planet will begin years before the crew even leave Earth. In the new 'low-cost' proposal put forward by NASA, three unmanned cargo missions will go on two years ahead. They will land a living habitat and an ascent vehicle on the surface, and place a ship for the return to Earth in Mars orbit.

When it is landed on Mars, the ascent vehicle will automatically begin to make its own fuel for the journey into Mars orbit. It will chemically combine carbon dioxide (CO_2) from the Martian atmosphere with hydrogen (H_2) brought from Earth to produce methane (CH_4) and liquid oxygen (O_2). This will reduce the amount of fuel needed to be shipped from Earth by about 30 tonnes.

When the crew of six arrive after a 180-day journey, they will land their crew module near to the habitat already on the surface. They will then move the two modules and join them together. For the following 500 days, these two circular structures, 7 m (23 ft) across, will be their home.

For the scientists on Mars, it will be vital to be mobile. If the surface is to be properly explored, the astronauts will have to spend hundreds of hours in their space suits and NASA has already designed a new lightweight Mars suit. But the most effective way to explore the surface of the planet will be by driving. Present plans suggest the crew could either drive around in a pressurised car, or they could use a remotely piloted vehicle controlled from the Mars base using a virtual reality headset. This second possibility would mean that a crew member could 'drive' the rover across the Martian landscape, examine interesting features and take samples of soils and rocks using a remote arm, all without ever leaving the habitat.

Once it has been proved that people can survive for long periods on Mars, a permanent base may become possible. This will use resources extracted from Mars itself.

Water is vital to human life, and can also be used to make hydrogen and oxygen for fuel. There is water on Mars, but at such low pressures and temperatures it can only exist as ice or water vapour. To get supplies of water, the colonists may need to 'farm' it from the land. A large area would need to be cleared of boulders and covered with a fine dust. Then a tractor carrying microwave heaters would move over the field, driving off some of the ice in the soil as water vapour. Fans in the tractor would suck up the air and condense the water.

As well as providing their own water, future colonists will have to manage their own atmosphere and eventually begin to grow their own food, until the base becomes largely self-sustaining.

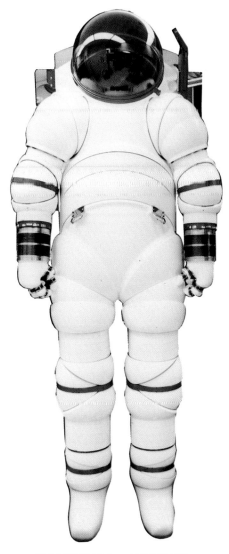

◁ *A prototype of a space suit suitable for Mars. Made of lightweight aluminium it would allow the crew to explore the surface for long periods.*

▷ *This pressurized rover would allow journeys of hundreds of kilometres across the barren surface of Mars.*

BIOSPHERES

IF WE ARE to colonise the Moon and Mars, we need to know how a sealed environment, far away from Earth, can be constructed and maintained. In 1991, four men and four women sealed themselves in a huge glass and steel complex, called Biosphere 2, in the Arizona desert. Two years later, they emerged having convinced many people that a totally sealed system can be made self-sustaining.

Biosphere 2 (Biosphere 1 is the Earth) is the dream of American ex-footballer John Allen. In the 1980s he teamed up with a Texan millionaire called Edward Bass to realise his vision. The idea was to build a totally self-sufficient living structure, sealed from the outside world, in which they could learn many of the lessons needed for living in an ecological way here on Earth, and for establishing bases on other planets.

△ Covering a huge site near Tucson, Arizona, Biosphere 2 was designed as a complete world within our world.

There are forerunners to Biosphere 2. The Russians built sealed experimental chambers called Bios 1, 2 and 3 as part of their space programme. In the 1970s, Bios 3 was sealed for six months with a crew of three inside, but it was not self-sustaining. While the crew were able to grow most of their food they did bring in meat for extra protein, and there was no method of recycling human waste. The greatest problem, however, was in maintaining a breathable atmosphere, and on several occasions oxygen had to be pumped into the chamber.

▷ A Russian biologist at work inside Bios 3, a forerunner of Biosphere 2. The Russian used knowledge gained here in designing their space station Mir.

Biosphere 2 is a vast project in comparison with Bios 3. It covers 1.27 hectares (3.15 acres), with 0.2 hectares (0.5 acre) of land used for intensive agriculture, and includes seven areas called biomes which have distinct climates: a rainforest, a freshwater marsh, a salt marsh, thorn scrub, a desert, and even an ocean with coral reef.

One of the major questions facing the Biospherians was whether they could grow enough food to sustain themselves for the two years. Over 80 species of edible plant were grown, staples such as potatoes, sweet potatoes and rice, as well as herbs, peppers, chillies, coffee and fruit. Nevertheless, lack of food meant the crew had to survive on less than 2000 calories day.

One of the problems was that the Biosphere was too shady. It was found that the structure was letting through 20 per cent less light to the crops than had been predicted. When this was coupled with an unusually cloudy period, it led to growth rates lower than expected, and a hungry crew – at least one unidentified crew member stole fruit from the stores.

▽ *The ocean and salt marsh 'biomes' inside Biosphere 2 hold nearly 4 million litres (900,000 gallons) of water. The ocean includes a coral reef and a beach.*

Managing the Biosphere's atmosphere was also very hard. After the Biosphere was sealed, the level of oxygen rapidly declined. The problem was based on a combination of factors. Firstly, micro-organisms in the soil were 'breathing' more oxygen than had been thought and producing carbon dioxide. Also, the concrete of which the Biosphere was built was absorbing the carbon dioxide at ten times the expected rate. This meant that the oxygen was becoming locked up in the concrete as carbon dioxide. As a result, oxygen had to be pumped into the Biosphere on two occasions.

Some commentators have criticised Biosphere 2 for the small number of research projects carried out during the first two-year 'mission'. But many lessons have been learnt about the problems of supplying the two most vital ingredients for life – food and air – within a sealed structure, and further missions are now being attempted. These experiments should undoubtedly help the designers of the first permanent manned bases on other worlds.

△ *NASA has built sealed living systems which might provide food and regenerate the air on the space station or a moonbase.*

MINING THE ASTEROIDS

A S WE EXPLORE further out into space, the amount and size of the hardware needed – spacecraft, rovers, bases – also increases. In the future, it will become more efficient and cost-effective to actually build these things in space. At first this will be done with pre-manufactured sections, but eventually there will be genuine manufacture from raw materials. These materials may be found on the Moon, but there is an even richer source of metals nearby in the solar system – the asteroids.

One of the few asteroids about which we know anything is called 1986 DA. It is about 32 million km (20 million miles) away in a 'near-Earth' orbit, and radar reflections have revealed it as as a lump of metal 1.6 km (1 mile) across. Estimates say it has one billion tonnes of nickel, 100,000 tonnes of gold and platinum, and 10 billion tonnes of iron. One day, asteroids like 1986 DA will be mined. They might even be towed closer to Earth so their enormous mineral wealth is closer to hand.

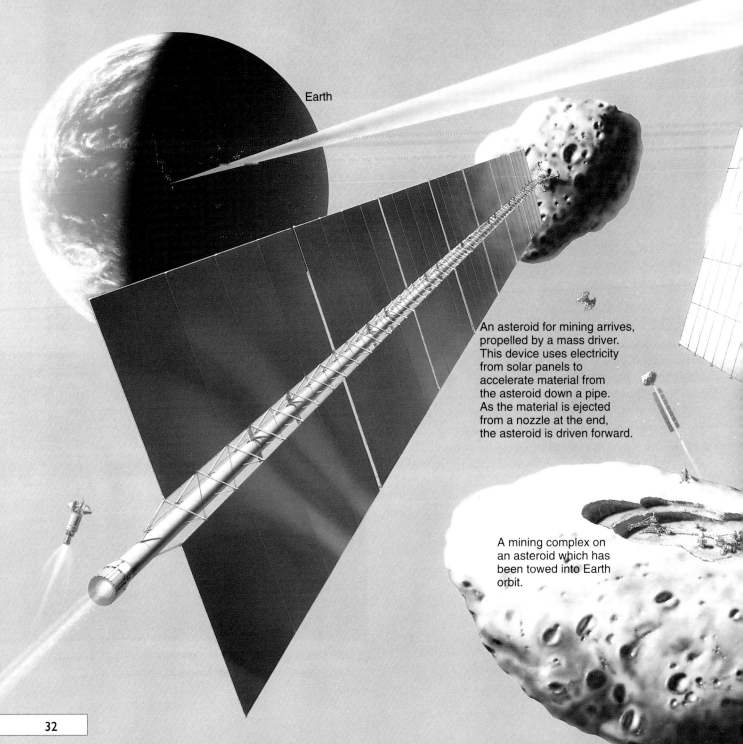

Earth

An asteroid for mining arrives, propelled by a mass driver. This device uses electricity from solar panels to accelerate material from the asteroid down a pipe. As the material is ejected from a nozzle at the end, the asteroid is driven forward.

A mining complex on an asteroid which has been towed into Earth orbit.

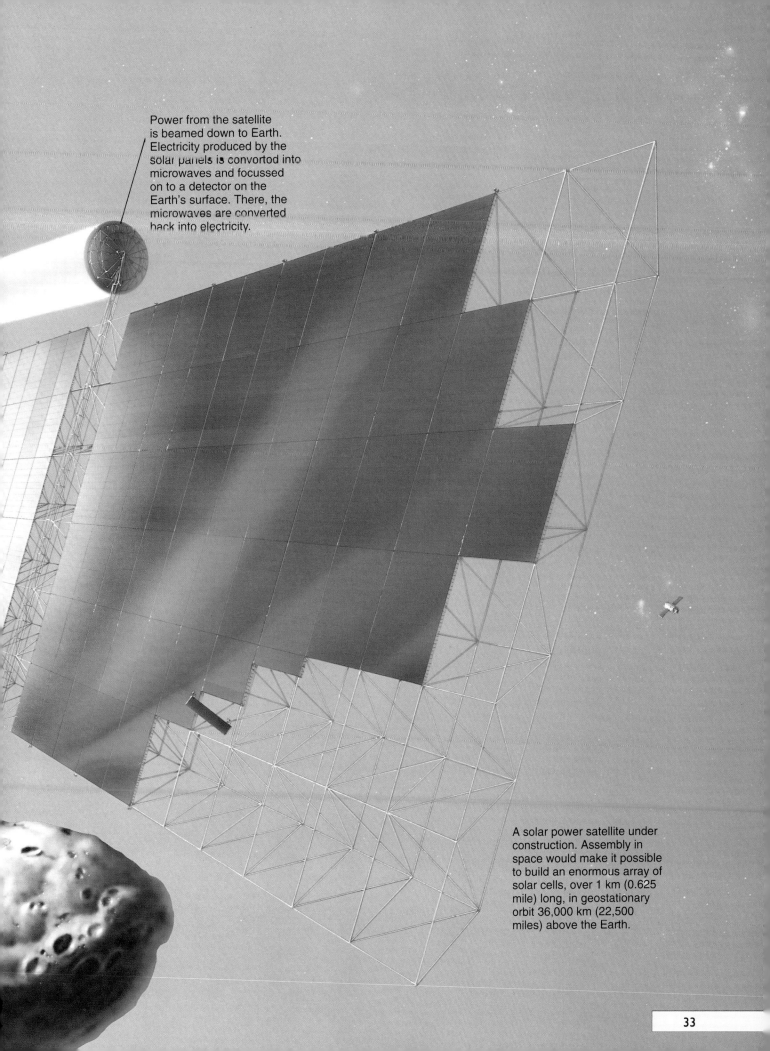

Power from the satellite is beamed down to Earth. Electricity produced by the solar panels is convertod into microwaves and focussed on to a detector on the Earth's surface. There, the microwaves are converted hack into electricity.

A solar power satellite under construction. Assembly in space would make it possible to build an enormous array of solar cells, over 1 km (0.625 mile) long, in geostationary orbit 36,000 km (22,500 miles) above the Earth.

AFTER MARS

TRAVELLING THROUGH the solar system from a base on Mars, there appear at first to be few places where a spacecraft could land. The gas giants Jupiter, Saturn, Uranus and Neptune are fascinating objects, but they have no solid surface. However, these enormous planets are surrounded by their own miniature solar systems – whole familes of moons. In 1610, Galileo was the first human to see a moon orbiting another planet when he detected four of the moons of Jupiter. Today we know of 12 further moons circling that planet.

In 1977, two Voyager spacecraft were launched by NASA to take the first close look at all the outer gas planets of our solar system and their moons. Both Voyagers visited Jupiter and Saturn, but Voyager 2 also passed close to Uranus and Neptune. The stunning pictures sent back by these probes revealed the moons of the outer planets as some of the most interesting objects in our solar system, and made them prime targets for future missions.

◁ The Voyager spacecraft carried two black and white cameras, but by using six movable filters the true colours of the outer solar system were revealed

Io is the most remarkable of Jupiter's many moons. If you were to stand on the surface of Io, you might think you had landed in hell. The surface is dominated by red and yellow sulphur which spews from giant volcanoes or spurts in liquid form from huge vents. These create giant plumes which can rise 300 km (188 miles) above the surface. The core of Io is made up of molten iron and sulphur, but the surface temperature is only –85°C (–121°F). This is cold by our standards, but it is uniquely hot this far from the Sun. In 1995, the spacecraft Galileo will arrive at Jupiter after a six-year journey from Earth. Unlike Voyager it will go into orbit around the giant planet. Its trajectory will take it close to the surface of Io and the other principal moons, giving it a unique view of the Jovian system.

▷ In this Voyager picture of Io, the giant scars of the only active volcanoes known beyond Earth can be clearly seen.

Titan, Saturn's huge companion, is the object in our solar system which is most like Earth. But it is not like the Earth of today, rather it is like the Earth of millions of years ago, just before life evolved. It may not appear to be at first, as its surface temperature is −180°C (−292°F). However, it appears to have a dense, nitrogen-rich atmosphere containing many organic compounds. This rich mixtures of organic molecules should make the evolution of life on Titan possible except for one thing: the absence of water in liquid form.

If you were to stand on the surface of Titan, it would be dark even in the daytime – only one-hundredth as bright as an Earth day. Methane rain would be falling from methane clouds, and above them a reddish mist of organic hydrocarbons would hide the weak Sun. But what would be beneath your feet is a mystery. The surface may be covered in an ocean of ethane, or it may be largely ice and rock. Voyager's pictures of Titan revealed little because of the dense atmosphere, but in 1997 NASA and ESA will launch the Cassini spacecraft. In 2004 this will go into orbit around Saturn, and a small probe called Huygens will separate and drop towards Titan. As it plunges through the atmosphere it will sample and test the gases, and as it hits the surface, its last message should reveal exactly what the surface is made of.

△ *After seven years of travel from Earth, Cassini will release the Huygens probe for its short journey through the atmosphere of Titan.*

Nearly 8 billion km (5 billion miles) from the Sun, is Triton, the largest moon of Neptune. Triton is very cold, with a surface temperature of about −235°C (−391°F), but the planet is far from dead. Standing on its frozen nitrogen surface, you might witness one of the strangest sights in the solar system – a geyser sending a plume of black material up 8-10 km (6 miles) above you. Just what causes these geysers is the subject of fierce debate. One of the most persuasive theories is that, during the day, the weak Sun penetrates the 1 m (3 ft) thick frozen nitrogen crust. This warms a dark layer just below the surface, and vaporises some of the frozen nitrogen. Then a huge blister, kilometres wide, rises up. Finally, it ruptures and a jet of nitrogen and dust blasts out of the fissure. Future missions to Triton would finally answer the riddle of what causes the plumes.

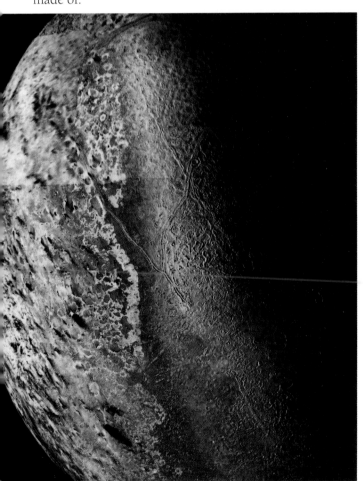

◁ *The surface of Triton is made up of a crust of frozen nitrogen, marked in places by mysterious black plumes.*

ENGINES IN SPACE

UNTIL NOW, most travel in space has used the same method of propulsion: a volatile gas or solid propellant is burned to produce thrust. But all combustible fuels take up a lot of room and weigh a great deal. They are quickly used up, and on a long trip the fuel for the return journey has to be carried as well. Other forms of propulsion will be needed for space travel to become routine around our solar system and beyond.

The next significant development in space propulsion will almost certainly be the nuclear-thermal rocket. This uses a nuclear reactor to heat a propellant such as liquid hydrogen. This technique has been used many times in space for orientating and positioning spacecraft, but not yet for powerful primary thrust. It is planned to use nuclear-thermal thrust for the journeys to and from Mars.

Another idea that is already being developed is electric propulsion. This too can use a nuclear reactor, or a huge array of solar panels, but this time to produce electricity and create a strong electric field. This in turn is used to accelerate ions of an inert substance such as xenon into a high speed jet at the rear of the craft. Although its thrust to weight ratio is low, an electric drive uses its propellant more efficiently than either a chemical or a nuclear-thermal rocket. It can continue accelerating slowly for years before running out of fuel, which make it ideal for cargo transports, and potentially makes possible manned journeys to the limits of our solar system.

▽ *In the 21st century, nuclear-electric propulsion may power cargo ships to Mars.*

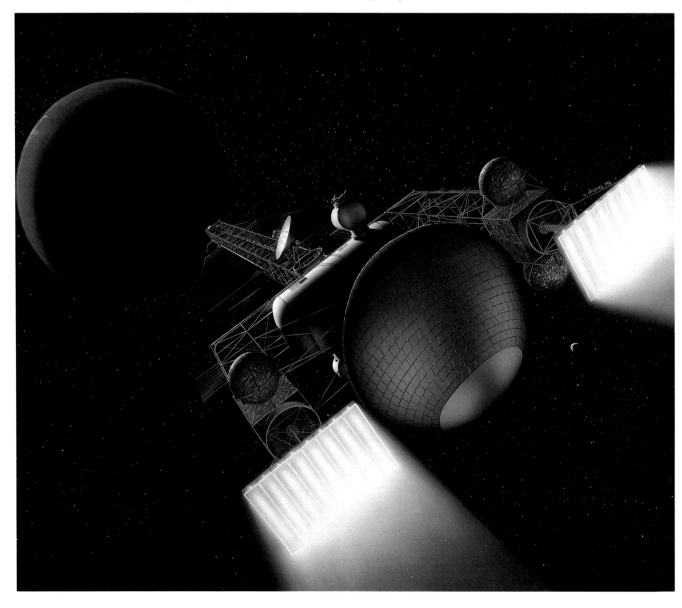

There are no winds in space, so sailing there may seem an extraordinary idea. However, there is the constant pressure of light from the Sun as it reflects off objects. In order for sunlight to carry a spaceship across the solar system, the area on which the sunlight can act must be large, and some designs for solar sails are 1 km (0.6 miles) across. A working solar sail could be steered by angling it in relation to the Sun, and while it might only accelerate by a few kilometres an hour, every hour, it would continue to do so as long as the sail was turned towards the light.

In 1992, the Russians flew the first solar sail in space, although sailing was not its primary purpose. Znamia or 'Flag' was a mirror 22 m (72 ft) across, intended to test the idea of reflecting the sunlight from space down onto the Russian Arctic during long, dark winters. Nevertheless, it was a space sail of sorts, being contructed of a thin layer of plastic with a coating of reflective aluminium.

▷ *Sailing across the solar system using a wind of light.*

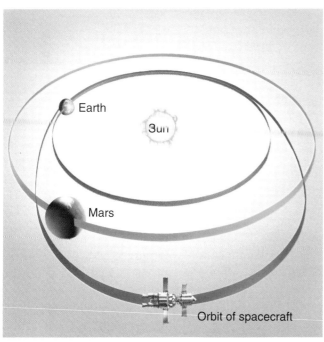

Earth

Sun

Mars

Orbit of spacecraft

If a permanent Mars base is ever established, supply vessels will need to voyage continuously backward and forward between the Earth and Mars. The most efficient way of running these ferries will be to put them into 'escalator' orbits. These are orbits which regularly cross the paths of both planets so that little or no thrust is needed once the orbit is achieved. Huge supply ships would pass by each planet, never stopping, on an endless round trip. To hitch a ride home, colonists would have to match exactly the path of the transporters as they passed by Mars, docking with them for the trip home.

◁ *Locked in escalator orbits, giant spacecraft circle endlessly crossing the orbits of both Mars and Earth.*

ALTERNATIVE EARTHS

ONE OF THE striking things about our solar system is that each planet is so different: fiery Venus, sleepy Mars, glorious ringed Saturn, gigantic Jupiter, and the frozen snowball Pluto. Such variation would seem to be the random product of events in the early history of the solar system. However recent computer simulations have shown that the shape of the system may be far from accidental.

Just after the Sun coalesced out of a cloud of gas and dust, the simulations show that there were numerous proto-planets lumps of rock up to a few hundred kilometres across. These sometimes crashed into one another, sometimes joined together, but finally they formed the planets we see today. What is fascinating is that the computer predictions all end up with a structure which is very close to the actual solar system. This would mean that, in other parts of space, where the conditions for star formation are similar, a solar system just like our own might emerge. In our galaxy alone there could be thousands of planets like Earth.

△ *The formation of our solar system from dust and gas may not have been as random as previously thought.*

△ *Terraforming for tens, or even hundreds, of years could make human life possible on Mars.*

For a planet like Earth to exist, the crucial factors are its size and its distance from the central star. In our own solar system, for example, Mars is a little too small, and Venus is a little too close to the Sun. But recently scientists have been exploring the possibility that both might one day be made more Earth-like. The process of turning a 'dead' planet into one where human life would be sustainable, is called terraforming.

Mars is the most likely contender. To terraform Mars, we would have to employ something that we are becoming familiar with on Earth – the greenhouse effect. The introduction of greenhouse gases, such as chlorofluorocarbons, to Mars on a vast scale and for hundreds of years, would result in the build-up of the greenhouse effect on Mars. This would warm the planet to near-Earth temperatures, melting ice at the poles and releasing carbon dioxide and water vapour from beneath the soil. Both carbon dioxide and water vapour are greenhouse gases, so the process would continue.

To support life, the temperature on Mars, – 60°C (–76°F) at present, would have to be raised above freezing so that water could exist as a liquid. But the atmosphere would still be largely composed of carbon dioxide. In order to create an atmosphere that contained something near the 20 per cent oxygen we have on Earth, genetically engineered organisms which could survive the extraordinary conditions (perhaps bacteria, mosses or lichens) would have to be introduced and then left for decades or hundreds of years to do their work.

Venus has the opposite problem to Mars - its incredibly dense, swirling atmosphere is mostly carbon dioxide. As a result it has a runaway greenhouse effect, pushing surface temperatures to nearly 500°C (932°F). But maybe even here it is theoretically possible to make the changes that would make it habitable.

Because it is so close to the Sun, the main problem is to reduce the sunlight hitting the planet. It may be possible to build a kind of giant sunshade in space, placed in orbit between the Sun and Venus. To convert the atmosphere, genetics would again play a part, engineering primitive plants and micro-organisms to consume the carbon dioxide and create oxygen. While theoretically possible, the scale of these tasks is so unimaginably huge that it is hard to envisage circumstances that would convince people on Earth to begin such a project. But, far in the future, those conditions might exist and new Earths could be created within our own solar system.

△ *Venus is almost the same size as Earth, but suffers extreme temperatures and 90 times the air pressure of Earth.*

▽ *A giant valley on the surface of Venus, pictured with radar by the Magellan spacecraft.*

IS ANYONE THERE?

IN 1901, Guglielmo Marconi sent the first morse code message across the Atlantic via his invention 'wireless telegraphy'. Marconi's message not only travelled across an ocean and triggered the age of communication, but also travelled into space, starting a one-sided conversation between Earth and the rest of the universe. Marconi's first morse bleeps will now have travelled a distance of close to 100 light years from Earth.

Since Marconi's first radio transmission we have been sending an increasing amount of radio, television and radar into space. This diagram gives an idea of the broadcasts they might be tuning in to in other stellar systems, if there is anyone out there to receive them.

▽ *There are now several hundred stars where it would be possible to have detected radio signals from Earth – if there were anyone there to detect them.*

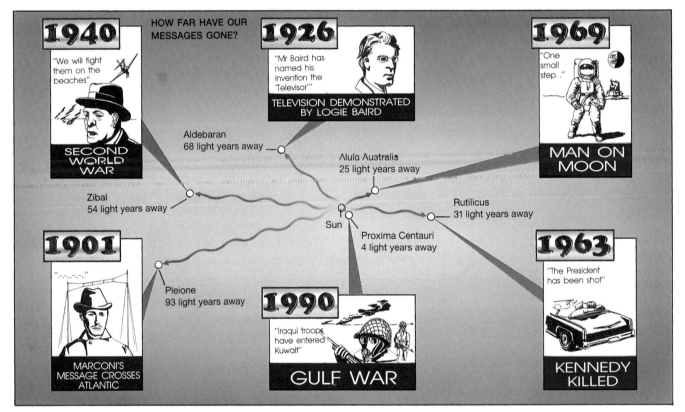

So how likely is it that there are other intelligent beings in the universe? The best estimates so far suggest that in our galaxy alone there must be many other civilisations, and there have been a number of attempts to communicate with them. In 1974, the giant radio telescape at Arecibo in Puerto Rico was used to transmit a message that included information about our solar system, the chemical elements important to life here, and the DNA molecule, the basis for most life on Earth. The transmission from Arecibo lasted just 169 seconds and was aimed in the direction of a star cluster 25,000 light years away, so perhaps it is not surprising that we have not had a reply yet.

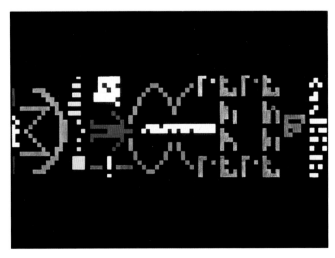

△ *The Arecibo message shows the shape of DNA, a human, and underneath the Sun and the nine planets of our solar system.*

◁ *The Arecibo radio telescope. Built to receive images of the stars, in 1974 it briefly became a transmitter.*

The most elaborate message sent into space travelled much more slowly than the Arecibo radio message. Aboard each of the Voyager spacecraft was a gold two-sided record on which had been recorded a huge amount of information about Earth. There was music from every continent, twenty-seven separate recordings in all, ranging from Mozart to Azerbaijani bagpipes. Greetings were spoken in 55 languages, and the sounds of our planet, from whale song to a space launch, were included on the disc. Voyager's record also included 116 pictures, coded into a digital form and then recorded. These pictures try to represent all aspects of life on Earth to an intelligence which has never seen it before.

▷ *Made of copper plated in gold, the Voyager record contained pictures and some of the sounds of Earth.*

Our attempts to send messages are unlikely to get an answer. The Arecibo message was transmitted only once, and the chances of even a remarkably advanced civilisation finding Voyager 1 or 2 are incredibly slim. So NASA has concentrated on looking for evidence of messages sent from other civilisations in the universe. Since 1960, there have been about 50 attempts to detect signals from space, but the Search for Extraterrestrial Intelligence (SETI) programme run by NASA is the most comprehensive. So far, despite a few false alarms, nothing has been heard. In 1992, the SETI project began listening in a region of the electromagnetic spectrum from 1 to 10 gigahertz. That region of the spectrum was chosen

because it is relatively free of interference. Using specially designed equipment that could analyse one billion bits of information each second, the search took two distinct forms: 1,000 specific stars were targeted for study using one radio telescope, while another searched the whole sky but at a lower level of sensitivity.

Unfortunately, towards the end of 1993 the U.S. government withdrew funding for the SETI programme as a cost-cutting measure. But at least some of the work will continue because since then $4.4 million has been raised from private benefactors such as science fiction writer Arthur C. Clarke. It seems that if we ever get E.T. on the phone, it will be a private call.

TO THE STARS

ONE DAY, probably in the next century, people will start to plan missions beyond our own solar system, across instellar space. As with space exploration since the 1960s, they will begin with unmanned probes. After that there will be pioneers who will wish to go themselves. But where will they be heading, and how will they travel?

The distances involved are vast even if exploration is limited to our own little corner of the galaxy. Our closest neighbours are the three stars of the Alpha Centauri system 4.3 light years away, and one light year is about 10,000,000,000,000 kilometres. At conventional rocket speeds the journey to Alpha Centauri would take 50,000 years. Interstellar explorers are unlikely, however, to be heading for the stars closest to us. Alpha Centauri is a triple star and probably has no planets – as the stars circle each other they would pull any planetary bodies which may have formed out of their orbits. Barnard's Star, our next neighbour, is six light years away, and is thought to have a family of planets. But it is both cool and very old – nearly as old as the Universe – and is almost certainly surrounded by dead worlds. We have to travel almost 11 light years from the Sun before we reach a star which may have living Earth-like planets. It is called Epsilon Eridani, and although it is smaller and younger than the Sun, it might well have given birth to life. But the most interesting of our near neighbours is one light year further away: Tau Ceti is of a similar age and size to the Sun, and there is evidence that it has a planetary system. Here there could even be intelligent life.

To reach any of these stars within a human lifetime will require propulsion systems capable of reaching enormous speeds. The British Interplanetary Society has designed an unmanned craft called Daedalus which would be driven by small fusion explosions. Tiny amounts of helium 3 would be ignited by a powerful electron beam. This would have to happen 250 times a second for years at a time, but they calculate that after four years the massive craft could reach a speed of about one-eighth the speed of light, 40,000 km (25,000 miles) per second. Even so, the journey to our nearest neighbour would take nearly 40 years.

◁ *After 40 years of travel, the Daedalus ship will have no fuel left to slow down, so it would pass through an alien system in a few hours.*

To go faster might need something which is even further in the future than fusion power: a rocket drive using anti-matter. Anti-matter has long been the stuff of science fiction, but it really does exist, and an anti-matter engine is theoretically possible. The idea is that anti-protons (the anti-matter form of protons) are combined with normal protons. When matter and anti-matter meet they annihilate one another but produce 'pions' – exotic particles with vast amounts of energy. These, it is thought, could be formed by magnetism into a jet which would propel the craft. In theory, an anti-matter drive would produce a thousand times the energy released in nuclear fusion, from the same mass of material.

But anti-matter is very hard to make, very hard to store, and very expensive. Current estimates suggest $8 billion per milligram, and an interstellar return journey at one-fifth of the speed of light would need 5,000 tonnes of fuel. At higher speeds an anti-matter rocket would need even more fuel, so it seems destined to remain just a theory for a very long time.

△ *A spaceship using anti-matter drive, capable in theory of approaching the speed of light.*

It seems probable that many of the early missions to the stars will have to be undertaken at slower speeds, and will not be accomplished within a human lifetime. Starships might set out on journeys destined to take a century or even longer. Some would be unmanned. But in time others could well carry people, enormous, ocean liner-sized craft would be self-sufficient worlds in which generations would live and die. If the history of human migrations is any guide, there would be no shortage of people wanting to set out into the unknown, knowing they could never return. These space 'arks' might make fuel stops at stars en route to their final destination. And so the human colonisation of the galaxy would have begun – and the vision of space as mankind's destiny, one of the driving forces behind crewed space flight, would have reached its logical and perhaps inevitable conclusion.

▽ *The Milky Way, an extraordinary sight in the night sky, is our home galaxy. The Sun is just one of a family of 100,000 million stars still to be explored.*

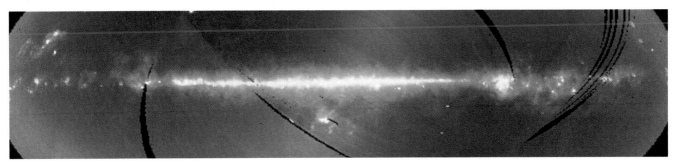

FACTS AND FIGURES

THE SOLAR SYSTEM

- The Universe is about 12,000 million years old and has hundreds of billions of galaxies.

- The Sun is one of about 200 billion stars in our galaxy called the Milky Way.

△ *The Sun photographed in ultraviolet light from Skylab, the first orbiting observatory launched in 1973. At the top is a rising column of gas called a solar prominence.*

- Our solar system is comparatively young, being only 4,600 million years old.

- Our solar system consists of 1 star (the Sun), 9 planets, 60 moons, several thousand minor planets, asteroids or planetoids, and several thousand comets. All 9 planets orbit the Sun.

- The Sun's mass is 333,000 times greater than that of the Earth.

- The temperature of the Sun's surface is 6000°C (10,800°F).

- The Sun is nine-tenths hydrogen. A fusion reaction in the inner core is converting the hydrogen into helium.

- The four planets closest to the Sun are Mercury, Venus, Earth and Mars. They all have rocky surfaces.

- The four giant planets Jupiter, Saturn, Uranus and Neptune have surfaces of frozen soupy gases.

- The shortest year (the time it takes to orbit the Sun) in the Solar System is on Mercury: It lasts 88 Earth days.

- A day on Venus is longer than a year on Venus. The planet spins on its axis once every 243 Earth days and orbits the Sun every 224 Earth days.

- The Earth rotates once every 23 hours 56 seconds – an Earth day. The Earth is orbiting the Sun at 29.8 km (18.5 miles) per second.

- Each year the Earth takes 0.0876 seconds longer to go round the Sun.

- The Earth gains 24 tonnes of space dust every day.

- The temperature of the surface of Mars is always below freezing. Average summer temperatures are −20°C (−4°F) at noon and −80°C (−112°F) at night.

- The largest planet in the Solar System is Jupiter. Its diameter is about 11 times larger than that of the Earth.

△ *Jupiter pictured by Voyager 2. The clearly visible Great Red Spot is an anticyclonic storm larger than the Earth.*

- Saturn is the only planet that has a density less than one – it would float in water.

- Uranus is spinning on its side.

- Neptune was the first planet to be discovered by mathematical calculation. It was predicted from irregularities in the orbit of Uranus.

- Pluto is the smallest planet in the Solar System with a diameter of less than the distance between Paris and Rome.

OBJECTS IN SPACE

- The world's first spacecraft to orbit the Earth was *Sputnik 1*, which was launched by the Soviet Union on 4 October 1957.

△ *Sputnik 1 was in orbit for 92 days. It was just 58 cm (23 in) in diameter.*

- The world's first communication satellite *Telstar 1* was launched by the USA in 1962. It carried the first live pictures from America to Europe and was able to handle 600 telephone calls at a time.

- Communication satellites are in geostationary orbits 36,000 kms (22,500 miles) above the Equator. They take exactly one day to orbit the Earth, and so appear from the ground to be stationary.

- *Viking 1* (USA) was the first space probe to land on Mars on 20 July 1976.

- The US *Pioneer 10* was the first space probe to Jupiter. It was launched on 2 March 1972 and flew past Jupiter on 3 December 1973 at a distance of 131,400 km (81,652 miles).

- *Pioneer 10* was the first probe to leave our solar system. It will never return.

- On 21 October 1975, the Soviet space probe *Venera 9* sent back the first pictures from the surface of Venus. The probe survived the ground temperatures of 2000°C (over 3600°F) for 65 minutes.

- The USA's *Voyager 2* was launched in 1977 and visited Jupiter, Saturn, Uranus and Neptune. Its voyage lasted 12 years and covered 6 billion kilometres before reaching Neptune.

- The largest telescope in orbit is the Hubble, which weighs 11 tonnes, is 13.1 m (43 ft) long and has a 240 cm (94$\frac{1}{2}$ in) reflector. It was launched on 24 April 1990 and cost $1.55 billion.

PEOPLE IN SPACE

- The first person in space was Yuri Gagarin of the Soviet Union. He orbited the Earth once in *Vostok 1* on 12 April 1961.

△ *Lt Yuri Gagarin's historic space flight lasted 1 hour 48 minutes. During the flight he was promoted to Major.*

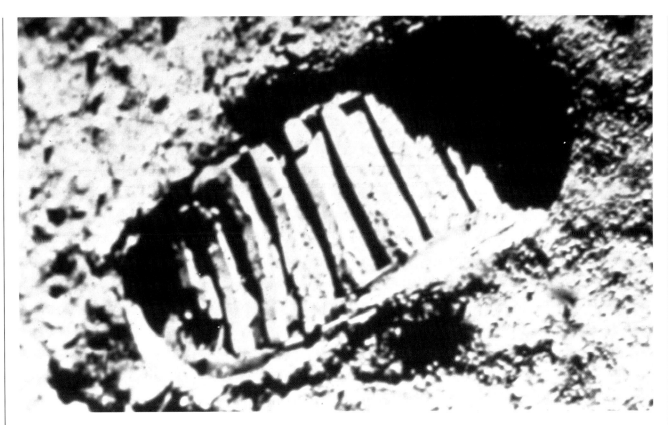

△ *Neil Armstrong's footprint on the Moon. No one knew in advance how deep he would sink into the dust*

- The first woman in space was the Soviet Union's Valentina Tereshkova, on board *Vostok 6*. She orbited the Earth 48 times in three days in 1963.

- The first people to travel around the Moon were Frank Borman, James Lovell and William Anders in *Apollo 8*. They sent back live TV pictures from lunar orbit 112 km (70 miles) above the surface.

- The first people to land on the Moon were Neil Armstrong and Edwin 'Buzz' Aldrin, who arrived in *Apollo 11*. Neil Armstrong set foot on the surface at 02.56 and 15 seconds GMT on 21 July 1969.

- Astronauts on the Moon weigh only one-sixth of their usual weight because of the Moon's low gravity.

- Only 12 people have walked on the Moon. They were all American men from six Apollo missions. They spent a total of 160 hours collecting 2,196 rock samples, which have been divided into 39,000 pieces and distributed to scientists in 19 countries.

- Earth's pyramids will erode away before the last footprints on the Moon, left by Eugène Cernan and Harrison Schmitt in December 1972.

- The longest time spent in space was by two Soviet cosmonauts, Musa Manatov and Vladimir Titov, from December 1987 to December 1988.

- The record for the greatest number of space flights is held by the USA's John Young, who has been on six missions. The first was in 1965 and the last in 1983.

- Astronauts in orbit can see 16 sunsets in one day.

- Astronauts eat 70% less food in space than they do on Earth.

- A person in orbit gets 2.5 cm (1 in) taller and 2.5 cm thinner.

- An astronaut ages less every day than someone on Earth by ten-millionths of a second, because of relativity.

- The first space walk was by Soviet cosmonaut Alexie Leonov on 18 March 1965. It lasted 12 minutes and he was attached by an air tube to the spacecraft *Voskrod 2*.

- The longest space walk was by Pierre Thuot, Rick Hieb and Tom Ackers on 13 May 1992 from the Shuttle *Endeavour*. It lasted 8 hours 29 minutes.

- The worst disaster on a space mission was on 28 January 1986, when 5 men and 2 women died on board the US Shuttle *Challenger*, which exploded 73 seconds after lift-off.

- The fastest speed at which humans have travelled is 39,897 km/h (24,791 mph), when the command module of *Apollo 10* was returning to Earth from the Moon on 26 May 1969. Thomas Stafford, Eugène Cernan and John Young were on board.

SPACE ODDITIES

- There are 3.5 million pieces of space junk in orbit, from old rocket boosters to flecks of paint, weighing over 2,000 tonnes.

- A single typing error caused the *Mariner 1* launch vehicle to crash into the Atlantic Ocean in 1962. Someone had typed a hyphen instead of a minus sign.

- A plus sign instead of a minus sign caused the Hubble telescope to point in the wrong direction in 1991.

- The first prize offered for communication with extraterrestrial beings was the Guzman prize announced in Paris on 17 December 1900. It was for 100,000 FF, but Mars was excluded because it was thought that contact with Martians would be too easy.

- The number of civilisations we might contact on other planets in our galaxy has been formulated by Frank Drake of Cornell University. The equation is

$$N = N_* \, f_p \, n_e \, f_l \, f_i \, f_c \, f_l$$

N_* is the number of stars in the Milky Way
f_p is the fraction of stars that have planetary systems
n_e is the number of planets in a given system that are ecologically suitable for life
f_l is the fraction of suitable planets on which life actually arises
f_i is the fraction of inhabited planets on which an intelligent life form evolves
f_c is the fraction of planets inhabited by intelligent beings on which a technical civilisation develops
f_l is the fraction of a planetary lifetime for which the technical civilisation survives
The answer to the equation is thought to be somewhere between 10 and 1,000,000.

◁ *More than six thousand bits of junk in low Earth orbit can be tracked by radar at the Space Surveillance Center in Colorado. Objects smaller than a grapefruit can not be seen, and include a wedding ring, a camera lens cap, and a screwdriver.*

INDEX